The Fundamental Guide to Mindfulness

How to find your Inner Balance and Way to Harmony
incl. Meditation Exercises & 30 Days Mindfulness
Journal

[1st Edition]

Thomas S. William

Table of Contents

Disclaimer 1

Introduction 3
    So, What Is Mindfulness..5
Chapter One: What You're Missing..**9**
    How to Start 12
    Bellows Breath..16
    Relaxing Breath 16
    Breath Counting..17
Chapter Two: Why Everyone Needs to Practice Mindfulness.19
    Why Everyone Can Benefit From Practicing Mindfulness......20
    The Main Reason We Need Mindfulness 22
    Phantom Symptoms 23
    Why Mindfulness is Needed...24
Chapter Three: Benefits of Mindfulness.................................**27**
    Mindfulness in Prisons..28
Chapter Four: Getting in Touch With Our Inner Selves **31**
    Set Up the Right Environment..35
    The Purpose of Mindfulness Exercises..................................40

Chapter Five: Taking Over the Robot..................................**43**

How is This Done?...45
Exercises That Rewire The Brain's Neural Pathways 45

Chapter Six: Connecting the Mind to the Body........................**49**

The Core Element in All Mindfulness Practice 50
Full Sensory Awareness 50
Mindful Listening 51
Mindful Smells..52
Mindful Sight..53
Mindful Taste 53
Mindful Touch..54

Chapter Seven: Stop Running in Circles...............................**57**

Conscious or Subconscious...58
Your Mind: If I don't wash my hands, I'll get sick.................61

Chapter Eight: Running Into the Fray **63**

The Three Breath Hug..64

Chapter Nine: Embracing the Good **67**

The Checker...68
Change Gears 68

Conclusion **69**

Journal Exercises **73**

Imprint...**105**

Disclaimer

The author's ideas and opinions contained in this publication serve to educate the reader in a helpful and informative manner. We accept the instructions may not suit every reader and we expect the recipes not to gel with everyone. The book is to be used responsibly and at your own risk. The provided information in no way guarantees correctness, completion, or quality. Always check with your medical practitioner should you be unsure whether to follow a low carb eating plan. Complete elimination of all misinformation or misprints is not possible. Human error is not a myth!

Introduction

From the time we enter into this world, we become constant thinking machines. Once that switch in the mind is turned on, it does not turn off until we take our last breath. So, when someone calls you a worry wart, or an obsessive worrier, they are usually not too far off the mark. It is perfectly normal for any of us to always be in deep thought. The real problem we should be concerned with is deal is not that we are constantly thinking but lies more in what we are thinking about and the way it is affecting our lives.

As we all struggle to navigate the many pitfalls of this ever-changing world, our thoughts can sometimes overwhelm us. All of us have daily fights with stress and anxiety about all manner of things. As a result, at times when you really want to quiet your thoughts and clear your head, they can resist and become even more intense. We worry about bills, what the neighbor said to us last week, what to feed our families, when we will find time to take care of our homes, and frankly, just how to get through each day of our lives.

When the regular struggles of life overtake us, our thoughts usually turn negative, which only adds to our normal level of anxiousness that we have to cope with. Few people realize that our thoughts are the instinctive triggers to our behavior. In fact, negative thoughts usually have a much larger impact on our overall physical, emotional, and mental well-being.

If you are one of those many people who tend to struggle with connecting to your inner person, you may only be vaguely aware of the constant dialogue that running through your head. Believe it or not, It is on all the time, whether you are awake or sleep. This dialogue, when healthy, reminds you of important matters like the doctor's appointment you have scheduled for later that day, it helps you remember the facts you have to learned for that test you have coming up, and it keeps you focused on your jobs so you can continue to bring home that paycheck and pay your bills. But when they take a negative tone, they become intrusive and begin to flow in a direction that leads to unwanted behaviors and habits. As a result, we find our minds flooded with a kind of background noise that crowds out all other positive and healthful thoughts that could lead us in a new direction.

On the surface it may seem strange that we have so little control over what flows through our minds but in reality, it is just part of our natural makeup. Think about all those sleepless nights when you couldn't stop the flow of negative thoughts that consumed you. It didn't what you did, there was no way to turn off the torrent. You ended up tossing and turning for most of the night until you finally fell asleep merely out of pure exhaustion, only to wake up the next morning, starved of rest, too tired to function normally, virtually guaranteeing you another day full of pitfalls and anxiety. Thus, you end up in a vicious cycle that feels almost impossible to escape from.

Learning mindfulness is a way to flip the script. Rather than allowing our thoughts to control us and dictate how we feel - it is a means of helping us to control them. Since we can't turn off this impressive thinking machine, we have to find a way to redirect it so that it works more to our advantage. Our thought process is essential for getting us through life. It is the one tool that makes it possible for making decisions, make plans, or set the kind of goals that give us direction in life.

In reality, it is not the fact that we think that causes us distress; it is the stream of negative thoughts that sits at the core of why many people feel unfulfilled in life. This negative thought pattern is usually the impetus that is behind our self-sabotaging efforts and is at the crux of those evasive behaviors that prevent us from taking life by the horns and living it to the full. In many cases, it is these negative impressions that lie at the core of our self-destructive behavior. It just makes sense then, that we utilize a strategy specifically designed to change those negative thought patterns so we can redirect our behaviors in a more positive way.

So, What Is Mindfulness

In the simplest form, Mindfulness is just a matter of making a point of focusing on your personal environment, both internally and externally. It is the active manner of choosing what elements as they play out in your life that you will pay more attention to. It comes down to making a conscious decision about how you choose to view your life.

While mindfulness originated with Buddhist monks more than 2,500 years ago, it should not be considered a spiritual or religious practice in any way. In the beginning, the Noble Eightfold Path (an ancient meditation practice often associated with mindfulness) has for years been thought to be the path to true enlightenment. But there are forms of meditation that have many practical applications for use in our own modern world that do not include elements of chanting, objects of veneration, or ritualistic maneuvers. For the purposes of this book, the techniques learned hear are in no way associated with in any semblance to a religious way of life.

No doubt, if you choose to pursue mindfulness outside of the religious spectrum, you'll come across some purists who will insist that the practice in a non-spiritual format is sacrilegious in some way. However, as you grow in your knowledge of the practice, you'll begin to discover it has many uses that can be applied to almost every environment and the positive results you will receive will not only be of benefit to the individual practicing it but also those who have to interact with them on a regular basis.

Part of the reason so many do not fully understand mindfulness is the varying definitions floating around. It seems that each and every person has their own conclusions about what it really is. For the purposes of this book, we will discuss the practice based on the following elements:

1. It develops one's ability to self-regulate their attention span and focus.
2. And it accepts a set orientation of the individual's experiences

One of the first things you'll learn about mindfulness is that our thoughts are actually the seed from which our behavior springs. When our thoughts turn negative, it affects our emotions. We feel terrible, which in turn causes us to react impulsively rather than with deliberateness. In essence, there is a direct connection between our thoughts and our feelings and another connection between our feelings and our own personal behavior. Therefore, mindfulness is a means of redirecting our thoughts so that we can have more positive emotions and take more positive actions. Of course, that is an oversimplified explanation of mindfulness and how it works. Later in this book, we will discuss these elements in more detail.

While anyone can benefit from practicing this age old form of meditation, it is especially helpful for anyone who generally find themselves:

- Trapped in negative thinking that is hampering their productivity.
- Often find they procrastinate to the point of losing time that could be spent on more productive activities.
- Struggling to concentrate and remain focused on important tasks.
- Are often frustrated by the excessive regurgitating of negative thoughts
- Struggle with stress, anxiety, or depression.
- Find themselves overwhelmed by life in general.

- Seek comfort in harmful distractions like alcohol, drugs, obsessive shopping, gambling, etc.
- Often find themselves out of touch with their world around them.
- Or just someone who simple wants to be more grounded in the world they live in.

There are likely many more reasons why you might benefit from practicing mindfulness and no doubt, as you go through this book, you'll come up with a few reasons of your own. Mindfulness is a means of reclaiming your life back and regaining control. Through the pages of this book, you will learn

- What you are missing in the world around you. When you find yourself trapped in an interminable mental loop, your brain is not processing the spirit of the moment you're in. With mindful practice you will increase your awareness of both your internal and external environment so that you can live more in the present and experience life as it was intended.
- Why everyone needs to practice mindfulness in their lives. We live in a world full of unexpected and unwanted pressures. Mindfulness is a way of separating and breaking free from the endless cycle of stress and giving you some peace of mind.
- The many benefits you will gain from practicing mindfulness, physically, mentally, emotionally, and creatively.
- You'll learn specific strategies that when implemented, will make it possible for you to get in touch with the person you are inside. You'll become better aware of what his happening in your own body, its purpose, and how to use that to take advantage of opportunities so you can get the most out of life.
- How to stop thinking and acting like a robot. You'll learn how to stop reacting to the world and approach life with a goal, so your life has a direction and a purpose.
- How to connect your mind to the body so that they work together rather than against each other.
- How to break the mental cycle that you find yourself trapped in.

- How to address your fears rather than hide from them. Rather than pushing your anxieties down deep into your subconscious mind, you'll be able to discover what is truly behind your negative fears and face them head on.
- And you'll learn specific strategies that will help you to force out those negative thought patterns and feelings that repeatedly come back so you can embrace much of the good that surrounds you every day.

Mindfulness will do more than redirect negative thoughts, when practiced correctly, you will find yourself with a brighter and happier future to look forward to.

At first, you may find that mindfulness sounds more like a Pollyanna way to address the negativities of life, but I assure you it is not. That is just your negative mind trying to get you to believe that you don't deserve a better life. In time though, you will discover a more balanced view of life in general. Together, let's learn just how to utilize the natural extension of our intuitive mind and put it to good use. It is a practice that is sorely needed in today's modern world. So, if you're ready for a change that will truly make a difference, it's time to learn a new way of using your thinking machine. It's time to practice mindfulness.

Chapter One: What You're Missing

The mind is an incredible device. If you are reading this book there is a good chance that you are experiencing times when the thoughts that pop in your mind often surprise you. You wonder, what made me think of that, or how did I come up with that idea. The brain is an amazing machine. In fact, it is the only machine in the world that can analyze itself and learn something new about it.

When working properly, the mind can open the door to some amazing opportunities. However there are often times when your mind can start to spiral out of your control. The human body, when under stress can affect the mind in very negative ways. This often happens, when a person experiences an overload of information coming in; the brain may struggle to process it all.

Think about it. There are five different ways that the brain receives data. Through sight, sound, smell, taste, and touch. You learned about these in your primary school days – the five senses. What you didn't learn then was that when the brain is receiving too much information at one time, it is forced to decide what is important and what is not. It will temporarily shut down some of the senses (or at least dim their receptors) so it can focus more of its energy on what it perceives as essential. We often call this condition "tunnel vision."

To enhance your ability to function, there are times when tunnel vision can actually work to your advantage. Artists often rely on this ability to help them to focus most of their energy on their creative work and business people tend to go into a zone so they can zero in on the task at hand. Sadly though, many people have been so overstressed in their lives that they are spending entire days, weeks, and even months in tunnel vision. It is those times when it can be more harmful to you than you might realize.

When you have tunnel vision, it means that one or more of your senses are shut down. In short, you have lost something called situational awareness, which can expose you to certain vulnerabilities. When you have tunnel vision you have a sort of hyper focus that can be beneficial in some cases. But quite often, when your tunnel vision is the result of negative thinking, it can actually diminish your productivity and effectiveness in many areas of life.

As an example of how this happens, think about driving home late at night. You're on a dark windy road and visibility is poor. Your concentration becomes more intense and soon you don't hear the music on the radio or any other noises in your environment. You are intensely focused on the road ahead of you. Add a thunderstorm to the equation and you probably won't notice anything else for the duration of your trip. You have heightened your sense of sight with tunnel vision and your auditory or hearing senses are diminished.

Actually, in some cases, one can literally shut off all of their other senses so they con focus. However, this can leave them vulnerable to a world of dangers and risks. Think about how this kind of mental process might be affecting your work, your family, and your relationships. While every situation of tunnel vision will not end up in danger, think how effective this technique can be at blocking out external data. You might miss the beautiful sunset that is dropping down just outside of your window, or you miss the birdsong that is playing right before your alarm clock goes off.

Because tunnel vision (at least the negative and more dangerous kind) is the result of stress, by practicing mindfulness you can regain your focus and literally reset your mind. As you enhance your skills in mindfulness techniques, your other senses will be heightened, and clearer thinking will develop.

One of the key elements of mindfulness is learning how exist only for the present moment. This will keep you more emotionally stable. When we are too keyed up, either in anger or fear, our brains automatically switch to the fight or flight state. When we do look around, we are more likely to see everything as a threat, even when no real danger exists. We find ourselves watching our backs, looking over our shoulder, and becoming overly suspicious about everything and everyone. This usually happens as a result of our need to focus on surviving. In this condition, we are not looking at the bigger picture of the world around us and we may find that we are missing something very important.

So, what are you missing in this mental state? One way to figure this out is to first learn how our brain responds when we are calm, and in a less stressful state of mind. In this state, a different area of the brain kicks into gear. This part of the brain heightens our focus in all of our senses. We are able to see opportunities as they really are. In this condition, we see the bigger picture; we still see the problems we have to face, but we are better equipped to identify the solutions that may be right in front of us. When we process our thoughts in this way, the world is no longer relegated to just the threat of danger, we can also see all the shades and variations of life around you. In short, we have a more balanced view of our world and we can cope better.

Understanding that when we are in a more relaxed state of mind helps us to see that we can be much more effective in life. Decisions are easier to make, we have less stress, and we are generally much better at interpersonal relationships. Along with an increased awareness of our surroundings, connecting us both with the internal and external influences of life, we are better equipped with the kind of mental faculties that will help us to analyze everything we are connected with from a more objective perspective.

How to Start

Interestingly enough, effective mindfulness starts with something that you already do about 20,000 times a day. For 99.9% of the population, it is an exercise that is done automatically. It is a natural bodily function that you do without giving it much thought. That is breathing.

It may seem strange to learn that the majority of people are not breathing correctly. This is because our brains are already programmed to adjust your breathing to give your body the exact level of oxygen it needs in order to function well for any activity you are engaged in. You don't wake up thinking about where or how to get your next breath. Your brain automatically adjusts your lungs for it. So, when you wake up, one of the first things you do is take in a couple of deep breaths and then you're on your way. But have you noticed how your breathing changes when you go for a jog around the block? No one plans on heading out on the path and figuring out just how much oxygen they need to take in or if they're going to stop along the way to pick up extra air; the brain automatically expands the lungs so you can take deeper breaths in order to send more oxygen throughout the body. Your muscles will need it.

Our bodies have already been impressively designed to naturally reach for what it needs. Nerves and other bodily sensors, like your taste buds, hair follicles, and those tiny little fibers in our ears and nose all send communications to the brains so that it knows how much oxygen your body needs to continue functioning in the current environment. That way, you slow down your breathing when you are not exerting yourself and it will automatically kick it up a notch when you need more exertion.

Breathing is also needed even if you are not physically active. Consider what happens to your breathing when you experience intense emotions. Think about how your breathing changes when you are angry, under stress, or afraid. Inevitably, your rate of breathing will increase causing shortness of breath, and when you are calm and relaxed, you are better able to take in long, deep breaths, which can relax you even more.

In the past, people were more physically active so nearly everyone that was fit had good breathing practices. Their busy lifestyles forced them to take deep cleansing breaths every day. In today's modern world though, the majority of us live pretty sedentary lives. As a result, most of us take shallow breaths that don't take in much oxygen. We sit behind a desk most of the day and we channel surf in front of the TV for the rest of the time. Both of these postures create an environment that restricts or limits the air flow into our lungs.

This problem is only compounded when we are under stress. The muscles of the thorax, (the part of the body that controls the heart and lungs) are responsible these vital organs will start to tense up and apply pressure, squeezing like a vice. This makes it difficult to breathe deepy so you end up spending your entire days just sucking up a limited amount of oxygen with each breath you take.

The first lesson in Mindfulness therefore, is to set up an environment where you can literally relax those muscles you can get a good flow of oxygen entering the body and the brain. Once you are aware of how your posture and breathing is affecting you, there'll be a noticeable difference that touches on every aspect of your life creating a calmer and clearer state of mind.

Follow these simple guidelines to adjust the way you breathe so that you can get better in touch with what is happening to your body.

1. **Adjust your sitting position.**

    Remember your childhood when your parents were constantly reminding you, 'Sit up straight! Don't slouch?' Chances are you probably grumbled and complained. It's true, slouching may seem to be more comfortable, but whether your parents realized it or not, there was good reason for them to teach you good posture.

    When you sit or stand erect, you are actually open up the airways in your diaphragm so that with each breath you take in the air can flow freely allowing more oxygen to get into the lungs. As you begin to analyze how you are breathing, start to take more notice of the changes in your body as a result of getting the extra dose of oxygen. You should notice the tension in different parts areas like your neck and shoulders begin to relax. So, try to make a conscious effort to breathe or push more air into those areas. As you do this, you'll notice your body begin to go into a deeper relaxation mode.

2. **Focus on breathing through your nose**

Concentrate on keeping the mouth closed so that the air flows through your nose. Your nose has been designed with a number of filters that will block impurities from the environment preventing them from entering the body. It is also much more in tune to negative influences than your mouth is. It can detect when there are poisonous gases, viruses, bacteria, and even extreme temperatures of the air. The tiny hairs inside your nose works as filters to block out these unwanted impurities so that each breath you take in is purer than any that come through the mouth. So, keep your mouth closed and concentrate on breathing through the nose.

3. **Use your abdominals**

Once you have mastered deeper breathing through the nose, you can enhance the breathing even further by engaging your abdominals. As you inhale, place the palm of your hand on your stomach so you can feel it expand and fill with air. As you exhale, feel as the stomach deflates as the air leaves your body. This will make you more aware This   of how your breath moves throughout the body and how it responds to the new infusion.

4. **Become aware of the different ways your body breathes**

We use the terms shallow breathing and deep breathing, but you may not know exactly what that means. In simple terms, shallow breathing is when you only breathe in enough air to fill the lungs and then you exhale. This is the type of breathing that most of us do as we go about our day. The air stops at the lungs and goes no further. Deep breathing however, pushes the air into the abdominal cavity filling the lower regions of the lungs and provides for more oxygen to be delivered throughout the body. There are several reasons why you might want to exert extra effort to do more deep breathing exercises.

A. It gives all the organs of the abdominals a well needed massage
B. It works to expel some of the toxins you've accumulated in the body
C. It relaxes the muscles and relieves stress
D. It can calm you down when you are agitated
E. It improves the digestive system
F. It enhances the cardiovascular capacity
G. And it helps to improve your posture

Once you have mastered the skill of controlled breathing, you are ready to apply some basic exercises that will help you to push out many of the negative thoughts that may be consuming you. The goal with the following exercises is to help you to make a connection to your parasympathetic nervous system (the part that controls your heart rate and boosts your intestinal and gland activity). By focusing your breathing on this area, you will be more relaxed with a calmer mind making it easier for your brain to be restored to a more normal and healthier function.

When you breathe deeply, you will be better connected to all areas of your body. In fact, your mind will be forced to turn internally so that it has to stop that constant inner dialogue that keeps running on a loop inside your brain. This will cause a physiological change called the relaxation response.

As you learn how to regulate your breathing better, you can then use it whenever you need to clear your head. Below are three different breathing techniques that have been very effective in relaxing the body and pushing out the stress.

Bellows Breath

1. Take several quick inhales and exhales through the nose. Keep your lips closed but relaxed and your breathing should be even. Each breath should be as short as possible. Don't worry about making noise in this exercise, it will get pretty noisy.
2. Make sure that you are breathingrapidly. Aim for three inhales and exhales for every second. This forces the diaphragm to respond quickly in and out giving it a good workout.
3. Repeat for five seconds and then breath normally for five seconds before going again. Try not to go for more than fifteen seconds the first time, but as you gain better control you can gradually start to extend your time until you can do this for a full minute.

When the bellows breath is done properly, you will feel invigorated. There will be a noticeable difference in your awareness of your surroundings immediately after you have completed the exercise. This is a great strategy when you want to boost your energy when you find yourself dragging around in the afternoons. So, rather than reaching for a boost of caffeine, try this exercise and you'll discover a healthier and more noticeable difference.

Relaxing Breath

When you find yourself getting nervous and jittery, try doing this relaxing breath exercise. It works like a drug in calming your nerves without the worry of possible addictions or dependencies. Its effects are subtle but after repeated practices you will start to notice significant changes. Use it whenever you feel distressed or anxious about something, but make sure to you time it so that it is before you react to the inciting event. You can even use it when you are having trouble falling asleep.

The relaxing breath, sometimes called the 4-7-8 exercise is very simple and requires no special equipment. That means it can be performed anywhere you are and any time you need it.

1. Find a good seating position so your back is straight
2. Push the tip of your tongue up against the ridge directly behind the upper front teeth and hold it there until you complete the exercise
3. Empty the lungs by making a full exhale through the mouth
4. With the mouth closed, take a deep inhale through the nose for four counts
5. Hold for seven counts
6. Do a full exhale through the mouth for eight counts

In the beginning you want to limit this exercise to only four breaths a day, twice in the morning and twice in the evening. You won't notice much difference at first, but after a few months of regular practice you'll start to notice a difference. It will improve digestion, lower your heart rate, and relax your muscles. As your body adjusts and accepts this new way of breathing, you can gradually add to the number of breaths for this exercise, up to a maximum number of eight breaths per session.

You might begin to feel light headed when you first do this type of breathing, but don't worry too much about it. Your body is just making adjustments. You may have to cut back your breathing count to two or three and build up to it, but if you continue regular practice of this, that side effect will eventually pass.

Breath Counting

This form of breathing is usually more challenging than the previous two exercises, especially if you are new but with practice you should be able to master it in a short amount of time. It will help to lower your stress levels, push more oxygen throughout your body, ease pain resulting from inflammation, and even increase blood circulation.

1. Start by sitting in a comfortable position that will keep the back completely straight
2. Tilt your head forward just a little bit
3. Keep your eyes closed and take in a few deep breaths through the nose

4. Allow for a natural exhale to happen for 1 full count
5. Take a second inhale
6. Exhale again for two counts
7. Repeat until you reach a count of five

This exercise helps you focus better and puts the whole body in a state of deep relaxation. For most of us, it is quite common for our minds to wander. When you notice that happening while breath counting, simply acknowledge those thoughts and continue with your breath counting.

For anyone who is practicing mindfulness, breathing is the most important part of every exercise. With proper breathing, you will be better able to focus your mind on the present moment. Because there is a direct correlation between mindfulness and breathing; it allows you to be more sensitive to the whole body making you more fully aware of what's happening internally as well as externally. Later, as you learn to follow the flow of air throughout your body, you will begin to recognize exactly how your body feels and will be able to actively control tensions, relieve pain, and stop anxious worrying on your own, without the need of medication.

Chapter Two: Why Everyone Needs to Practice Mindfulness

For those who are unfamiliar with the practice of mindfulness, its value is often under rated. They automatically dismiss it as one of the odd eastern practices of an ancient world. However, those people have yet to learn the true value of getting to know their inner selves.

We live in an extremely complex world that is moving at a pace never before seen in mankind's history. When you learn to practice mindfulness, you learn how to stop and take notice of everything that is happening all around you. You learn how to look at the world as a third party and can see just how its events are affecting you. Mastering this technique is at the core of claiming your life back and getting the control you need.

If any of us are not focused, life in general could quickly pass us by. We lose out on wonderful opportunities that we can grow from. These losses may leave is with feelings of regret and inhibits our freedoms so we fail to live up to our full potential, or even cause us to live a life of basic existence where we are barely getting by.

Mindfulness helps us all to look keenly at our world and root out those things that are interfering with what is most important. So, rather than living as a number in this new technological age, only seeing what our tunnel vision allows us to see, we can experience life as it was meant to be. Recognize our place in the big picture and cut through all of the expectations and stereotypes of this world.

Of course, those are the psychological benefits of practicing mindfulness. Once we learn how to put our lives on pause and find that sweet spot within ourselves, we'll also reap the physical, spiritual, and emotional benefits as well.

You can look forward to an improved emotional intelligence and an enhanced brain function. The more conscious you are of your surroundings, the more sensitive you will be to the stimuli your brain receives. This will not only apply when you interact with your inner circle of friends but will also be at work in other environments. Imagine how an enhanced brain function will serve you on your job. As a result, you will be more creative and more in tuned with what you can do for others within your circle.

Why Everyone Can Benefit From Practicing Mindfulness

Even though cultural perceptions have cast a pale shadow on those with varying emotional disorders, practicing mindfulness will give them better control over their behaviors so they can manage their responses to uncomfortable stimuli they receive from their immediate environment. There are other advantages that the average person could find just as rewarding if not more so.

You become a better listener: When you learn how to be present in the moment, your mind is less likely to drift into other areas. You'll find that you are not easily distracted or you're not focusing on what you want to say next. This alone will strengthen your relationships and enhance your ability to open up and allow more people to enter your life.

You'll learn how to see things from a different perspective: Mindfulness opens your mind so that you are better able to look at situations from all angles. Rather than having a narrow focus and seeing things as one-dimensional, you'll develop the ability to analyze situations from all angles. This will equip you to become a better decision maker and to remember to take a minute to look beyond the obvious.

It helps you to be a better communicator: When you are able to identify your emotional triggers and recognize the cause, you will be more open to talk about them. This knowledge not only helps your awareness of yourself, but also gives you more empathy for others. You'll know how to talk and relate to other people on a deeper and more meaningful level than you might have before.

You'll develop more appreciation: Once you learn to slow down and stop the busy cycle you're caught in, you'll start to recognize your accomplishments and the contributions that others have given to you, you'll start to appreciate the people in your life for all they have done for your benefit.

You'll have more peace of mind: For many people, mindfulness gives them a sense of inner peace. So, rather than spend the bulk of their days reacting to every tiny little disturbance to the point that they never seem to be able to relax they find an inner calmness that allows them to approach every situation with a sense of deliberateness. Sometimes, the anticipation of something happening can add enough stress to one's life that the negative event you're expecting doesn't even have to happen for you to lose control.

Having more peace of mind is not just about getting through the day and avoiding pitfalls. It also allows you to relax enough so that you can get the sleep you need at night. And the sleep you do get will be sweeter than you can imagine. Rather than having a fitful night in expectation of what will happen or regretting what did in the past, you'll be able to drift off into peaceful slumber getting a full night's rest. The next day, you'll be more alert and on point with all your tasks, which will automatically make you feel even better.

You'll be able to overcome your fears: All of us are afraid of something. Whether it's a fear of spiders or of speaking in public, many of those fears are not founded in reality. Through mindfulness, you'll learn how to challenge your innermost fears, look at them realistically, and determine whether or not they are based in reality or are a fabrication of your imagination.

Through mindfulness, you begin to see where you are in life, what is getting in your way, and develop strategies to change your circumstances. In short, as your awareness of how your life is unfolding and developing, the better able you will be to regain control.

Of course, no one's life will ever be one-hundred percent perfect, but we can all do with a little improvement in at least some of these areas, if not all of them. So, you have a choice here. You can continue pushing through each day fighting a constant barrage of stress and all the negative thoughts along with it, or you can embrace life and live it so that it brings you peace and joy, by just learning how to connect to your inner person and map out a new future for yourself by practicing mindfulness.

The Main Reason We Need Mindfulness

One thing we all have to live with is stress in our lives but that doesn't mean that stress is always a bad thing. When stress is healthy, it can motivate us to make that extra push towards something good. It can keep you grounded when you go on a job interview, it can move you to do your best on an exam, or it can jiggle your nerves just enough so that you can speak in front of a crowd of people.

More often than not, however, stress can be very negative leaving a painful impact on your life, at times in ways you may never have noticed. You may not realize it, but anxiety and excitement evoke the exact same reactions in the body. The only difference is that one (anxiety) is based in fear or dread while the other (excitement) is based on hope; one negative and one positive emotion. Both also have the same core element, stress.

According to the American Psychological Association, stress is a perfectly natural reaction to stimuli. For example, ask yourself how you usually feel when you find yourself in a stressful situation. Maybe you're going on a first date or you're sitting in a theater watching a scary movie. In either of these situations, the symptoms are the same. Your heart will start to pound, your knees may get a little weak, your palms begin to sweat, or you start to have trouble breathing.

These are automatic responses that have been experienced by people of every generation since the dawn of mankind. It is an inborn reaction that was built in to protect us from anything that would be a possible threat to our lives and well-being. They are automatic because in the face of eminent danger, we may not have the luxury of time to think about and analyze our situation. If we're being hunted by a man-eating tiger, we don't want to waste time thinking of our options. Instead, the primal center of our brain quickly acts so that our bodies recognize the danger immediately. Our system is then flooded with a concoction of hormones that send signals throughout our bodies making it possible for us to have an appropriate response to the threat without the need to take the time out to carefully analyze it. This usually means an elevated heart rate, an increase in blood pressure so that you are prepared to deal with the threat.

Under ideal circumstances, all of this is good, but we live in a world that has us undergoing constant and unrelenting stress. You are probably not worrying about getting eaten by a predator, but the same anxiety associated with earning a paycheck that doesn't cover the bills evokes the same kind of response. As a result, when under stress, your body can fall into an endless cycle of defense mechanisms. It's like an old phonograph record with a scratch in it. It keeps reacting to the same scenarios over and over again never giving you any relief. If this is allowed to continue indefinitely, the damage goes beyond a few little jitters but can have a major effect on your overall health.

Phantom Symptoms

There may be times when you don't recognize that you're under stress. The absence of symptoms does not mean that you're not feeling the effects. Many people are running to the doctor with complaints of headaches, stomach pain, indigestion, heart palpitations, and other phantom symptoms that seem to have no apparent cause. With each passing day, reports show that more people are getting through each day relying on sedatives, anti-depressants, anxiety medications, and pain relievers with no end in sight.

When the stress is chronic, the symptoms become even more serious. Without relief, stress can interfere with every aspect of your life. The longer it lasts the harder it is to recover from the problem. Complaints of fatigue, lack of focus, irritability, and more are common. In some cases, it has even been known to open the door to a wide number of diseases. For example, increased stress has now been found to be a contributing factor in cardiovascular disease, cancer, and asthma. This is only a beginning of the list of the possible detrimental effects associated with chronic stress.

Why Mindfulness is Needed

Part of our stress comes from living within the confines of cultural norms. Our minds are cluttered with unwritten codes of laws that dictate what the world expects from us. This kind of indoctrination starts when we are very young and is compounded with each societal group we belong to. Think about all the expectations that you are required to meet. On any given day, you may be judged by others based on your role in the family, your position at work, any organizations you belong to, and your social and economic status in life.

Yes, many of these stressful events are just part of living in this world. They may be important elements essential for maintaining a cohesive society and order, but it can be overwhelming at times, especially if they are coming at you from all directions.

Since it is not likely that the world will take a step back in time to the simpler lives of the past, we have to learn how to deal with stress in a more practical and realistic way. This is where mindfulness can play a part. The strategies you will learn here in this book will be tools you will turn to frequently to give you the relief you need. With these techniques you will learn:

- What is causing your stress
- How to interact with people on a more positive level
- How it gains better control over your emotions
- How to be proactive when faced with a stressful situation rather than reactive
- And know when to seek additional help when it is needed.

Once you learn these things, you will start to observe gradual improvement not just in lower stress levels, but physically, emotionally, and psychologically as well. You'll notice that your thoughts will flow more freely, your creativity will come back and the real you will begin to shine through all the clutter that has been blocking your mind.

In fact, over the last few decades, mental health professionals have effectively used mindfulness-based interventions to treat a wide range of disorders both mentally and emotionally with some pretty positive results. While the results can vary, just by virtue of changing your relationship with your own inner thoughts there have been some pretty impressive results. It has been used to treat some extreme cases of PTSD, anxiety and depressive disorders, and OCD.

According to one study reported on in NCBI, it "suggests promising evidence for use in treatment-resistant depression, in people with current symptoms of anxiety or depression, including those currently depressed and suicidal."

This is a good time to point out that mindfulness is just one way to address these types of health problems. In some cases, the condition could be so deeply embedded in an individual's subconscious, that they may need a more aggressive approach to managing their problem. Some may need professional treatment, medication, or other therapies in order to find relief.

It is also important to note that mindfulness is a proactive activity. It will not work if you only read about it. It is the active part of the therapy that will help you. Those who are not willing to do the exercises listed here or in any other material on mindfulness will not see the results that so many are reporting on. However, if you are committed to doing the work and being completely honest with yourself, it is quite realistic to expect to reap many positive rewards and find yourself living a whole new life that will bring you joy for many years to come.

Chapter Three: Benefits of Mindfulness

More evidence supporting the benefits of mindfulness can be found in a report released in the Harvard Business Review. Over the years, there have been a number of extensive research studies where the practice has been thoroughly examined. One of the primary reasons for this close examination is that they have recognized that many people who have sought treatment for anxiety or depressive disorders do not always respond to the mainstream forms of interventions and treatments. Their goal was to examine mindfulness to determine if it was a possible alternative approach for those who were unable to respond to the predominant form of treatment.

The results of their studies have demonstrated a vast array of benefits both physically and mentally. On the physical side, many participants in the studies reported relief from conditions like irritable bowel syndrome, psoriasis, fibromyalgia, and chronic pain. On the mental/emotional side, they reported relief in less anxiety, depression, and post-traumatic stress disorder. The results showed that at the very least, mindfulness was on par with a number of other treatment methods.

They tested their hypothesis that mindfulness could relieve these symptoms not just by the word of each of the participants but also by looking at the brain itself. Each participant was put into a scanner where researchers could actually observe the activity of the brain while they were asked to perform specific tasks. The purpose of the scans was to see if the thought processes inside the brain had changed after they had received mindfulness training.

While in the scanner, participants were asked to complete two different tasks, one that was designed to increase their awareness of their bodies by concentrating all of their attention on how their hearts beat, their breathing, etc. The other task required them to reflect on specific phrases that were similar to their own internal voice that only they could hear inside their heads. The phrases were the common negative phrases that most people say to themselves. "I am a loser," and "I can't go on" and "who do you think you are?"

After listening to these comments, the participants were asked to stop thinking about them but then to address the thoughts that were triggered in their own minds. The results of the study, concluded this year (2019), show that regular practice in mindfulness (over a period of eight weeks) showed that there were some differences in how the amygdala responded to certain stimuli. The amygdala, an area of the brain known to be important for emotions, had experienced some changes. According to Athinoula A. Martinos, the author of the report, it was the very first time they could scientifically prove that meditation like mindfulness could actually affect the emotional processing center in the brain even after being in a meditative state. Over the years, more studies have also been conducted supporting the same results.

Mindfulness in Prisons

Another amazing revelation about mindfulness are the numerous studies that have been conducted on young men who have been incarcerated over the years. The studies were done on those who had problems with impulsivity and trouble controlling their emotions. The studies were conducted in several different cultures, such as those done in Chinese prisons and in other facilities that housed incarcerated youths. While the studies did meet with some challenges in regards to implementation and getting the inmates to want to participate, the results turned out to be quite encouraging.

At the Oxford Centre for Mindfulness, for example, Mindfulness-Based Cognitive Therapy or MBCT was found to be effective in lessening the amount of recurrent depression experienced by some inmates. Those who experienced three or more depressive episodes over a 12-month period, saw a good 40-50% drop after going through a program of mindfulness.

The same evidence was revealed in other studies as well. The University of Surrey published the following results:

1. 63% drop in depression
2. 58% drop in anxiety
3. 40% drop in perceived stress

The most impressive evidence was that the inmates were able to maintain their level of success over a three to six month period by continuing to keep up with their mindfulness practice. While there were some challenges in motivating the prisoners to participate in the exercises, those that did found that by learning more about their internal thinking patterns, they were better equipped to redirect their negative behavior and therefore adjust how they interacted with other people. In addition to the lower levels of anxiety, stress, and depression, there was a general consensus that their overall well-being was more positive.

The advantages to this can be far reaching. Once one understands that their well-being is not some elusive expression but is actually a combination of several factors including the mental and physical health and their level of happiness and overall satisfaction in life, they can then see how their actions are not in isolation but are an extension of a complete package. They could appreciate how identifying these elements can have a profound effect of their whole life experience.

Many believed that the practice actually gave their lives a sense of meaning, something that they had struggled to find before.

It is clear then that everyone can benefit from practicing no matter where they are in their lives. While some people may have mental and emotional imbalances that require more extensive psychological treatment, the majority of us, even those who are getting by on a seemingly normal existence can benefit from developing a more positive view of life as a whole. Whether you just want to have a calmer state of mind or you're in search of making more drastic changes to your personality, it all starts with one single step that can lead down a completely different path. So, if you're ready for that kind of change, let's get started.

Chapter Four: Getting in Touch With Our Inner Selves

It is easy to tell someone that they need pay attention to the world they live in. Parents everyday are constantly reminding their children to look both ways when crossing the street, watch out for strangers, and be diligent in performing their chores. It's pretty easy to say these thing, but with all the activity going on around us, it is another thing entirely to put into practice.

Our lives demand that we focus on many different things every day, but when you first start to learn mindfulness, you need to start by tuning all of those things out and pay attention to one very important person. Yourself.

Mindfulness starts out simple enough, but for many people it may be the hardest lesson they have to learn. It requires each individual to first learn how to show love to themselves. Self-love is difficult, because our lives are played out in a world bent on constantly telling us that we are not worthy, that we have somehow failed in some way or have been found lacking we convince ourselves that we don't deserve any love.

We may not say or think these things out loud, but often it is a recurring thing in the minds of many. The problem with this kind of internal dialogue is the belief that it fosters. Generally, what we say to ourselves is what we believe and if we believe we are not deserving, even if we attempt to change our behaviors or do anything to change the negative feelings we have, our inner critique will sneak in at some point and trigger self-sabotaging behaviors just to make sure we don't get what we're striving to achieve.

You may attempt to do a better job at work, you may try to get in a little exercise or eat more nutritious food, or you may even attempt to heal a bad relationship, but somewhere along the way, that little voice will always be there, constantly needling you to go against what you're trying to do.

So, how do you start to change this dialogue so that you can show yourself a little loving tenderness. It starts by making some conscious choices. First, you need to create a division between yourself and that inner critic that's interrupting your life.

If you haven't realized it by now, there is more than one voice that is talking to you inside your head. You've probably realized that sometimes there is a conversation that is going on and you're just observing the dialogue.

No one has been able to determine the precise moment their subconscious gets its voice, but most would agree that up until that point, they were quite carefree without many inhibitions if any at all. Watching children at play, you can easily tell which ones have their inner voice turned on and which ones do not. When that inner critic springs to life, they become self-conscious, nervous, and fearful of many things. It has been described as a criticizing commentator that is passing judgment on every action they take.

When you listen to that voice, your actions no longer become spontaneous. You find yourself caught up in a constant stream of thoughts that interrupt your sleep, disrupt your concentration, and may even cause you confusion. Some people's inner critic is so loud that they it can become a mental health issue. However, hearing voices in your head does not necessarily mean that something is wrong. In most cases, these voices are perfectly natural. Whenever you're not focused on something specific, your mind is immediately flooded with thoughts and ideas. It may be thoughts about future events, or they may be remembrances of things in the past.

Your thoughts are actions just like everything else you might do. If they are frightening you then chances are you haven't realized that just like your body's muscles and tissues, you have the power to control them. But until you learn how to do that, your thoughts will continue to run rough shod through your mind, whether you like it or not.

It helps to understand how the thoughts you may be experiencing can differ from one another. For example, a real or a concrete thought is one that you consciously make. It is usually based on your ability to evaluate certain situations and form a conclusion. We all think along these lines every day. We contemplate our problems, formulate plans, and make decisions all without much worry. It is because of this type of thinking that we are seen as rational creatures and it is this thought process that separates us from animals and other creations.

Real thought connections may seem random but they do have a pattern to them. For example, you might be thinking about where to go on your vacation and your thoughts may drift to some of the places you've visited before, then it may move over to an article you read a few years ago about a remote island that you had never heard of, then a line in that article may cause you to recall the lyrics of a song you heard when you were a child, which will make you think of that creepy uncle you used to hate, to a lesson you want to teach your son. As you can see, it may seem random and confused, but each thought directly connects to another.

The problem comes when these thoughts are flooding your mind so quickly that you find it difficult to concentrate on one thing for very long. These thoughts are fueled by all the images, impressions, and information your brain accumulates and comes from your conscious mind. It is your active brain processing loads of data it is receiving from your five senses and trying to make sense of it all.

However, while all of those thoughts spring from our conscious mind at work, it is more than one voice in your head that is voicing its opinion. In fact, there are several other types of voices, all speaking over each other and trying to get your attention.

Intuition: All of us have a little tiny voice that instinctively recites to us a moral code that dictates right and wrong. This is that inner voice that we turn to when we are trying to make a decision. Your inner voice will warn you when you are facing danger, when you're about to make a mistake, or when something doesn't feel quite right. It is a strange phenomenon that we rely on when we find ourselves in unfamiliar situations.

The intuitive voice is instinctive. It means our survival and it is at the very base of our existence. No one questions the importance of a life of meaning and purpose. No one had to learn that, it is part of what makes each of us uniquely human. Everyone has a natural talent or inclination towards certain things and we want to optimize these ideas and make them a part of our lives. This is what gives us an unique identify that defines who we are. However, the subconscious mind also has its own voice, and this voice is usually that inner critic that is disrupting the flow of the intuitive mind.

You can think of the conscious mind like the waves of the sea. They continue without letup and are never ending. You can focus on any number of these thoughts any time you want. They are real and visible to you. Your subconscious mind, however, can be likened to the current that moves those waves in one direction or another. This is the natural order for how the brain works.

Like the waves of the sea, your conscious thoughts move in the same direction. You set your goals and dreams on these waves and as long as your inner voice stays out of it and doesn't try to move you in a different direction, you will have smooth sailing. However, the mind often works against your natural flow of thoughts. It flows in many different directions, often contrary to what you really want and hope to do.

The pressure of these inner thoughts is not necessarily based on fact. Instead, it is based on perceptions that may have been picked up throughout your life. It remembers the harsh words of a disappointed parent; it recalls the failed grade you got when you were twelve; and it remembers the numbers on the scale after you've had that triple chocolate cheesecake last night at dinner. It remembers all of your failures of the past and it won't let you forget them.

When both minds work in harmony, you have a nice healthy relationship with yourself. You can make wise decisions, set goals and stick to them, and are usually working at your best no matter what your abilities are. But when your two minds are pulling against each other, you can find yourself in a mental tug of war. One mind says yes you can while another mind is trying its best to convince you that you can't.

Set Up the Right Environment

We've already determined that you can't turn off that voice. It is constantly playing like the buzz of white noise in the background of your thoughts and will never stop. However, what you can change is what that voice is actually saying to you. You have to heal the relationship you have with yourself and change that dialogue to a more positive one.

When you first start, you may need to create an environment that is conducive to meditation. This doesn't need to be an elaborate shrine that you escape to, but you will master the skill much quicker if you have a safe haven to develop your skills. In the ideal environment, you will find it much easier to relax and allow yourself to let go of your anxieties so you can concentrate on changing your inner voice. Below are some basic guidelines that will help you to choose the right place to practice your mindfulness.

- Choose a space with no distractions. Make sure to avoid that could pull your focus away from meditation. This includes, computers, televisions, cell phones, or anything else that could cause you to lose your focus on your goals.

- Eliminate as much noise as possible. When meditating, keep the windows closed, especially if your space will be in an area where there is a lot of traffic, children playing in the street, or noisy neighbors. If you have children or pets ,make sure that your space is set up so they can't distract you.
- Some people find it easier to relax when there is music in the background. If you're one of them, be careful of the type of music you play. Don't go for the latest hit songs, but choose something that will be soft, soothing, and leave you with a peaceful feeling.
- Fill the room with fragrances. You might try burning incense or candles scented with essential oils. Essential oils have their own healing properties so the right one could be the perfect solution to help you to get into a relaxed state much quicker.
- Find a comfortable place where you can relax. Whether you choose to meditate in a seated position or lying down, you have to be comfortable. You don't want something that is too hard, but you also don't want something that is too soft. If you decide to meditate on your bed, you don't want a mattress that is so soft that you are sinking while you're trying to focus. On the other hand, you don't want a chair that is so hard that you can't get comfortable either. If you plan to sit on the floor, it might be a good idea to put down some cushions or something soft so that you can relax and focus on your meditation rather than on finding the right position.

There is no need to buy special or expensive equipment. Unlike other forms of meditation, you won't need any alters, to recite chants, or ring bells, chimes or any other instrument. All you need is a quiet, comfortable place where you can be alone with your thoughts and you're all set. Now, let's get to work on changing how your mind works.

There are several basic steps involved in this process.

- Identify the dialogue
- Analyze it
- Change the conversation

Let's focus on step one: identify the dialogue. Have you ever been in a crowded room or auditorium and heard the buzzing of conversation all around you? What happens when someone comes up and speaks to you amidst the din of noise? Most of us will struggle to understand what is being said. Even if you strain to hear every word, the surrounding noise drowns out any hope of conversation.

In order to identify the dialogue that is constantly running through your head, you will have to develop a strategy for drowning out all of the out outside noise so you can focus clearly on what is being said. That way, when there is no other sound except for the voices playing out in your mind, you'll be able to finally hear clearly what your inner voice really believes about you.

This starts with the breathing exercises we discussed in Chapter Two. After you have been practicing these techniques for a while, you'll develop the skill of turning off the noise anywhere at any time, but in the beginning, you'll have to find a quiet place so you can concentrate.

After you've done your breathing exercises for a few minutes, you'll notice the tension leaving the body and you start to relax. Take the time to relish in this feeling. Appreciate the fact that you are finally alone. Then start the process of identifying your thoughts.

- Concentrate on your heartbeat. Feel it's rhythm and concentrate all your thoughts on it.
- Allow everything around you to fade into the background until you can only feel the rhythm of your heart and how it matches with your breathing.
- Recognize and feel the body's automatic functions as they respond. Feel the vibration of the air as it is drawn in and out of your lungs. Feel how the muscles are rejuvenated as the blood carries oxygen to each cell in your body.
- Don't rush this process. Rather take your time and explore all of the sensations you're feeling.

You may be surprised when you discover that you can tap into all of these feelings. We all know that all of these things are happening inside you every day, but it is another thing entirely when you can concentrate enough on this natural flow of energy to be fully aware of it.

Now, let your mind drift to the constant stream of thoughts. This may seem a little strange at first, but keep in mind that you are not there as you, but are merely an observer to see how your mind is processing things. As a neutral party, you can do this without judgment. You have enough of a negative judge in your own thought patterns. Just observe the type of thoughts your mind is feeding you. Then observe how you react emotionally to those thoughts.

This can be an intriguing phase because up until this point, you have quite likely begun to realize that your emotions and feelings are not knee-jerk reactions to external stimuli, but that your mind has been feeding into them all along.

This is the identifying phase of mindfulness. You can't address any behavior until you can clearly see where the triggers are coming from. If your thoughts are negative, then your emotions will also be negative. Use the following steps to address this type of thought pattern.

1. When you recognize a negative thought, stop.
2. Take a few cleansing breaths and remember that you are a neutral party and are only visiting as an observer.
3. Observe the moment and watch how your body reacts to the thought.
4. Take notice of the emotions that come up in response to the thoughts
5. Stop and make a decision
   a. Now you have a decision to make. If the inner critic is negative, then you have to actively decide to ignore it.
   b. You may also choose to challenge it, forcing your critic to give evidence of its conclusions.

It may feel a little odd to do, but some people found it's easier to identify this critic better if they give it a name. This gives it its own unique identity giving you the freedom or permission to separate yourself from its influence. This makes it easier for you to identify the point when negativity starts so you can turn your back on it.

Now, as these negative thoughts begin to come up, start to challenge them. For example, if your negative thoughts begin to question whether you deserve a raise on your job, challenge the idea.

Thought: You haven't done anything to deserve a raise.

Challenge: Yes, I have. I wrote that proposal that got the company a new contract

Thought: You are not as pretty as you think you are.

Challenge: So, what? Beauty is different for everyone.

Thought: You can't speak in public.

Challenge: I haven't done it yet, but I have the skills.

Thought: You're too fat.

Challenge: Why does it matter?

For years, your inner critic has been having a one sided conversation, without ever being challenged. By identifying these thoughts and then challenging them, you are pushing your brain to not automatically accept them as a matter of fact. The challenges require that your conscious mind give evidence for its conclusions. In reality, more often than not, these assumptions made in your mind have been rooted there since childhood, and you've never truly reasoned on them or looked at them in a logical manner. The result of this type of analysis will almost always reveal some assumptions that have been automatically accepted in your life.

The Purpose of Mindfulness Exercises

Mindfulness is done in phases. It is not that you will sit down and all your inner thoughts will be instantly revealed to you in one sitting. It is something that you will have to work at. The longer you practice it, the more will be revealed to you.

Observation: When you observe in mindfulness you are doing more than just watching what's going on inside your head. To observe, you need to connect to your senses. So, while you are listening to the dialogue that is going on, you also want to get in touch with each of your senses. Take note of everything you see, taste, smell, touch, and hear without reacting or making any form of judgment.

This is not as easy as it sounds. Throughout our lives, we have been expected to label everything we see. In time though, you will develop the skill of being in the moment without the need for labels or judgments and just learn how to experience the bare sensations you are receiving.

Awareness: In the next phase, you will become aware of all of those senses. This is a little different from observing what's happening in your environment, because you will now decide to accept it and recognize it for what it truly is. In other words, you'll be tightening your focus and bring yourself more in-tune with what you observe.

The majority of us go about our daily activities without much thought as to what is happening all around us. We are buried deep in our own thoughts and ideas. Our minds are constantly adrift jumping from thoughts of the past to thoughts of the future. These thoughts are often clouded with regrets, painful memories, or dreams of things to come. But with awareness, your focus will be on what's happening in the present moment. The past is gone and the future hasn't happened yet. What matters most is what's happening now.

Being awake and being aware are not the same. When you are awake, you are simply not in a sleep state. You may not be dreaming but you still may not be in touch with the here and now either. It takes conscious effort to be aware of what's happening around you at any given point in time.

Listening: Mindful listening is different from your usual listening habits. When you are engaged in normal listening, it is easy for the mind drift off topic to other things. This is perfectly normal behavior, it's just what the brain does. However, when you are practicing mindful listening, you will have to remain in the present so that you can absorb everything that is being said.

It will take time to develop this practice. By acknowledging that your mind has drifted and then bringing it back to the moment, eventually, you'll learn to concentrate your efforts and energy on hearing everything being said in your environment.

Mindful listening is also about reserving judgment and not formulating opinions or thinking about how you will respond. It all directly relates to the main point of mindfulness; living in the present. In other words, you are paying purposeful attention to whatever is happening at that precise moment. It connects well with your heightened sense of awareness of your surroundings and everything that is happening within it. The main purpose of mindful listening is to slow down your inner dialogue so that you can receive the messages you were meant to receive.

Immersion: Mindful immersion is to bury yourself deep within the moment. Regardless of what you do, make sure to give your undivided attention to the task at hand. If you're alone, pay focus intently on the sights and sounds that surround you. No one lives in complete silence and you'll be surprised at what you hear when you open your mind to it. If you're studying, it's developing the habit of fully engaging in the subject and focusing on the task in front of you. If you're engaged in conversation with someone else, it means fully immersing yourself in that person's message, ideas, or lessons.

Appreciation: The final stage of mindfulness is that of appreciation. It will be a natural evolution of your total experience. It is the culmination of developing awareness, honing your listening skills, and being able to immerse yourself in the moment. Once you have achieved these skills, you will naturally develop a deeper appreciation for everything in your life.

A natural extension for developing this appreciation is that you will find yourself with a deeper sense of belonging. And once you feel a part of something bigger and more important than yourself, you will begin to build a deeper sense of trust. Think about it. Our negative thoughts usually foster a spirit of suspicion and fear, which automatically encourages separateness. But as you immerse yourself in the world, you'll become more a part of it and your trust of yourself and others will naturally grow out of that.

As you can see, mindfulness is far more than sitting back and listening to your breath. On the surface, it is a simple matter of training your mind to focus, but deep underneath this simple explanation, mindfulness taps into every core of you being and teaches you how to get the most out of life rather than exist in this hectic world.

Chapter Five: Taking Over the Robot

All of us have gotten stuck in a never ending repetitive thought pattern that literally drives us to distraction. You remember that song in your head that you couldn't stop thinking about. Or perhaps you continue to relive an embarrassing moment that you never seem to get away from. Maybe even years later, that event pops back in your head and for some reason you can't shake it.

For most of us, these kinds of recurring thoughts are nothing more than an irritation. Something that annoys us and drives us into a very unpleasant place in our minds. However, for others, the thoughts are so invasive and so distracting that it literally interrupts our lives. Either we are incapable of creating harmony in normal society or it disables us in extreme ways and we find we are unable to function at all.

Mindfulness is an effective way to reduce those thoughts and in most cases, stop them in their tracks. But before we get into how this works, let's analyze just how the brain processes what's really happening in our minds.

Our brain's are divided into two hemispheres. The left side (or the left hemisphere) is where we get our logical and analytical thinking and our right hemisphere is where our creative genius comes from.

This is where our perceptions of the world around us are formed. When these two hemispheres work together, we can live an enjoyable and balanced life. Our bodies are in harmony with everything around us.

What brings us out of balance is usually the demands of the world around us. In the past few decades, creativity has often been discouraged and presented to young minds as purely a waste of time. Schools have gradually reduced the study of the arts and have leaned more heavily towards analytics like math, science, programming, etc. This has presented generations of people who are focused almost entirely on these sciences creating a world void of emotional expression. The focus is on "doing" something rather than "being" someone. Creativity is an inherent part of all of us. After deprogramming by society, many become convinced that they do not have any sense of creativity, but that is never the case. If you have a right brain (which all of us do) then you possess the ability to be creative. Just like that inner voice in your head, society has told us it's not important, therefore many have missed their opportunity to develop that side of who they are.

When the world in general is pushing for only left-brain activity, the right-brain tends to go dormant. Practicing mindfulness can help us to reactivate our right-brain and allow more of our creativity to flow through. This will help to slow down the constant chatter in our heads and break free from the endless loop that is driving us to distraction.

Keep in mind that even with mindfulness, it is often difficult to break free from obsessing over somethings. Remember that it is the observation and the noticing of the activity of our minds that will be the first step into bringing our thoughts back into harmony with the balance that will eventually make the shift in our brains. Each time we do this, we reinforce the neural pathways that will eventually get strong enough to break the pattern.

It is by challenging these preconceived beliefs that it is possible to over time, restructure our neurons and create entirely new thought patterns.

How is This Done?

The part of the brain called the amygdala is directly associated with our emotions and our base fears. This area is what kicks into gear when we are faced with a threat; it triggers our fight or flight response. When our mental state is in an obsessive mindset, it is the amygdala that goes into overdrive. However, after completing an 8-week mindfulness course, researchers have discovered that the amygdala begins to shrink. At the same time the brain's pre-frontal cortex (the part that is responsible for our awareness and decision making processes) actually gets larger. After years of research through the use of MRIs, we now know that this is not an occasional event but is in fact, a common occurrence in those who frequently meditate. As a result, those who do meditate are better able to maintain a balanced stream of thoughts when faced with difficult situations.

What generally happens is that the connections between these regions start to get stronger and they begin to work more in sync with each other. The more you meditate, the areas responsible for your attention and concentration begin to strengthen. The extent of these changes is directly correlated with how much time you dedicate to mindfulness meditation. In essence, the more you meditate, the more higher-order thinking prevails and the primitive, knee-jerk reactions of fight of flight weaken.

Exercises That Rewire The Brain's Neural Pathways

Exercise #1: Hand Exploration

Of all the parts of the body, the hand can reveal more about the inner you than you might realize. Believe it or not, they work in complete harmony with the different hemisphere's of the brain and are capable of starting a dialogue between them that can bring about balance. This exercise will require you to first get pen and paper so you can take notes on what you observe.

- Examine your dominant hand closely and write down ten characteristics that you notice.

- Repeat the exercise by observing ten characteristics of your weaker hand.
- Compare the two lists and analyze the differences.

By following this exercise, you will begin to notice specific patterns that you may have developed. It will reveal your perceptions of the world around you. For example, if the two lists are significantly different then it likely portrays how your two hemispheres are not working in sync with each other. But don't just stop there. Ask yourself why they are different and then go in a little deeper. Look inside yourself to see what emotions are evoked by this new knowledge that you have gained.

As you analyze, make sure that you remain completely objective. This is how you will get honest answers to what's really going on inside of your brain. Remember the pattern is first observation and then awareness.

Exercise #2: Create a Dialogue Between Your Right and Left Brain

This exercise also requires you to have pen and paper. You won't necessarily have a verbal dialogue, but you will have a written one.

- Start by using your dominant hand to write a question. The question could be about anything; problems you have struggled with, relationships with others, or performance at work.
- Answer the question by using your weaker hand. Your answers can be anything related to the question. You may recall something from your childhood, a poor decision you might have made in the past, and examine the alternatives you could have used.

You will be surprised what this exercise will reveal to you. You may even learn more about your body than you realized. In fact, some have described the results as having a sort of out of body experience. Your body is a memory machine and believe it or not, all the answers you seek are already there. The reason many of us realize it is because both sides of our brains are completely out of sync.

Exercise #3: Visualization

Visualization is a powerful tool when it comes to mindfulness. This is looking at your environment through the mind's eye and not relying entirely on the what the physical eye actually sees. For this exercise, you will be primarily accessing the right brain to help you through this. Remember, it is the right brain that has been pretty much dormant with most of us, so getting it to function may seem a little awkward at first, but in time, the practice will become much easier.

- Start by sitting in a comfortable position and cupping your hands together in your lap
- Examine how your hands fit together:
  * If the right hand is cupping the left, it shows a more masculine perspective
  * If the left hand is cupping the right, it shows a more feminine perspective
- Examine how you feel about this dominance – Does it feel good to you or are you feeling a little discomfort with this realization. Do you feel a preference for one particular side?
- Now, take notice of your posture:
  * Are you sitting up straight and erect or are you leaning more to one side? Which?
  * As you notice these imbalances, make a conscious effort to bring everything back in harmony physically. These imbalances are subtle signs that mirror what is happening in the brain. Accept them, and then slowly start making it a habit to adjust your body to be more in alignment.
  * Visualize your body working in harmony.
  * After meditation, start to focus more on what your body is doing as you go about your daily routine. Notice how your body naturally moves in a certain way, and start the process of making adjustments.
  * Finally, change the speed in how you do things. Maybe slow it down or try to speed it up and then gauge how these adjustments make you feel.

If you continue these practices, over time, you will begin to notice that your body will take on a more balanced way of functioning. Practicing these exercises gives you the ability to gradually move from that instinctive knee-jerk reaction to taking a more decisive role in your life. In time, you will begin to recognize just how mindfulness can equip you to become more proactive in life rather than reactive.

Chapter Six: Connecting the Mind to the Body

In the last chapter, we learned how to use mindfulness practice to bring your mind into harmony with your body. By doing this, you can easily bring more balance into your life, which will automatically bring you more calmness and a higher level of peace.

In this chapter, we can do the same with other parts of the body. As you have probably been able to see by now, mindfulness is about being keenly aware of everything your five senses absorb. Remember, that it is only through these senses that your brain receives any input about the external or the internal world that you live in. The more conscious you are of these elements and the more aware you are of the affects they have on you, the easier it will be to navigate through them so you can find a happier and more content lifestyle that isn't saddled with negative thinking and unwanted actions that are crippling your progress.

The following exercises are simple but will bring positive results. There are five different senses so we'll introduce five different exercises that will enhance each to get you started on connecting to your whole body.

The Core Element in All Mindfulness Practice

No matter which sense you want to connect to, mindful breathing always comes first. We've already learned a little about proper breathing in Chapter Two, but here are a few more points that will help you to fine-tune your breathing when you are about to engage in some of the mindful practices. On average, we all breathe in and out about 20,000 times each day. We do it without thinking, but there are a number of things you can do that will help you to enhance your experience:

- While you can breathe anywhere or at anytime, when practicing mindfulness you'll get better results when you're sitting in a meditative position (on a chair or on a floor with your back straight).
- Start by taking slow, deep breaths, not shallow ones that only fill the lungs. Focus on expanding the belly, too.
- Inhale through the nose and exhale through the mouth. Focus on getting the breath to travel through your whole body.
- Get a steady rhythm going.
- With each breath out, try to clear your mind and let go or at least slow down your train of thought. You can do this by concentrating on just your breathing to start.
- Continue to do this until you feel your body begin to relax.

Now, you are ready to tap into your senses and step into some mindful connectivity exercises.

Full Sensory Awareness

Once you have mastered breathing in the comfort of your mindfulness space, you can freely take it on the road with you. You can do this while you're driving home in traffic, as you go about your daily activities, even when you're preparing dinner with your friends. It will help you to become more in tuned with the world around you. In fact, it is recommended that you try this in as many different places as you can to help you to learn how to connect on many different levels.

- As long as you are in a safe place, take the time to stop and carefully look at your surroundings. You are paying deliberate attention to your environment.
- Go through each of your senses one at a time and become aware of all the messages the senses are picking up.
- Ask yourself how these stimuli are making you feel. Are you getting excited, tired, depressed, or bored.
- Make a mental note of these feelings without judgment and then immediately start to focus on the next sense.

The more you do this exercise, the more you'll learn what is triggering your stream of emotions and your behaviors. As you do, you will begin to realize just how to adjust your thoughts to bring more calm into your life.

Mindful Listening

Mindful listening is listening with a purpose. It is different from hearing in the sense that you are just receiving information because it is in your environment. You are making a conscious decision to listen to the things around you. You are opening up your ears to certain sounds (in this example to music) as a means of clearing your mind of any preconceived ideas you may have influencing your judgment.

- Start by choosing a musical piece that is unfamiliar to you (one you've never heard before)
- Make sure you're wearing your headphones as you listen to shut out all outside noises
- Close your eyes to shut out any visual interference
- Listen to the song and visualize yourself on a journey
- As you listen, try to single out each sound you hear: the voice of the singer, the musical instruments, the speed and pace of the song, or any other acoustical elements
- Don't think or analyze the song but instead analyze how it makes you feel.
- Later, you can determine why it makes you feel that way and make adjustments by challenging negative thoughts that may come up.

Your goal is to use a piece of music that is as neutral as possible. Choosing music that you are emotionally attached to will only add clutter to your mind. Finding something that you are unfamiliar with will help you to relax and activate a different center of the brain. It will also help you to clear your head of negative thoughts so you can focus on the music itself.

Mindful Smells

Our sense of smell is one of the most powerful senses we have and is often underrated. While our it is not as keen as most animals, there is no question that this sense can evoke powerful emotions. Our olfactory senses are very closely linked with our memories often more than the other senses. How many times have you passed by a bakery and immediately thought of something from your childhood. Or perhaps you were walking along and caught a scent that immediately instilled fear into you.

Smells are so closely related to your emotions that the entire perfume industry has succeeded based on this very fact. What you smell can evoke powerful emotions. So, it just makes sense that if we are better in tuned with our sense of smell that we are more likely to connect with our environment on a much higher level. We may find that it is our sense of smell that is directing our behavior more than our sense of sight or hearing.

- After doing your breathing exercises begin to turn your focus towards your sense of smell
- If you're at home, try to detect some foods that may have been prepared earlier in the day. Can you distinguish the smells of certain foods? Very few people have trouble identifying the smell of bacon cooking or the scent of a roast in the oven. But try to sniff out less obvious scents like rice cooking in the pot or last night's casserole.
- After food, try to identify other smells that are in your environment. Can you catch the faint scent of your shampoo or the smell of your fabric softener.

- If you are away from home, try to close your eyes and catch the scents that are wafting in the air. Electronic equipment, automobiles, and even different stores have their own unique scent.
- As you pick up each scent, try to place them in different categories. Some scents you will find pleasurable and others you will find offensive. Try to determine why you feel that way and take note of which ones evoke powerful emotions in you.

Mindful Sight

When using mindfulness for your sight, you need to focus your attention on your immediate environment. Take extra time with this exercise. You don't want to just see your surroundings, you want to examine them carefully, looking for the smallest of details. Take extra notice of the objects, the colors, shapes, and how they make you feel.

Colors can be categorized as warm or cold. As you study your environment, which colors dominate the area and what emotion comes out. Is there an absence of color and why is that color missing?

Then turn your attention to your physical body. Notice the contours of your shape, the lines in your hands, the texture of your hair. Take the time to soak in all of the details of your environment and examine them to see how each one makes you feel. This exercise will reveal just how what you see on a regular basis is affecting your own personal behavior.

Mindful Taste

Surprisingly enough, you don't have to eat anything to do this exercise. However, if you are new to this, it might make it easier to if you have something to drink or eat.

- Start by focusing on the sensations inside your mouth. Take notice of how the tongue feels, its thickness and its weight as it sits in your mouth. Think about what tastes are still lingering on your tongue and how the saliva feels as it rolls over it, washing away any remaining residue from your last meal.

- Take the tongue and run it over each of your teeth one at a time, then move it along the inside of your cheeks and notice the different textures that are there. The softness of the cheeks pressed against the hardness of the teeth. Feel the upper ridge behind the top teeth and the soft upper palate right behind it.
- If this is too hard for you at first, then take a sip of something or take a bite of something and notice how your mouth awakens and comes to life with thousands of tiny taste buds sending messages to your brain.
- Ask yourself how certain foods make you feel and then try to figure out why.

Mindful Touch

Finally, you want to connect with your sense of touch. The same general rules apply. You first want to observe what you feel and then after you have identified all of the minute details, Take note of the type of emotions or thoughts they are producing.

- Start with your hands palm up on your thighs. How do they feel? What physical sensations are you feeling? Maybe it's the roughness of your jeans, the suppleness of the skin, the smooth or roughness of the fabric, or just your own body heat.
- Extend your awareness beyond your hands. After you have analyzed everything that your hands feel, turn your attention to your feet, where you are sitting, whatever is touching your skin.
- Ask yourself how does your body respond to these touches. Do they tense up from the cold of the metal chair? Does it pull towards the warmth of the heater? Can it relax on the pillow you're sitting on? A deeper analysis will help you to learn what is behind the tension and stress you are feeling.

Understanding your body and how it responds to this type of stimuli can teach you loads about yourself. As you grow in your awareness of how your body communicates you will be more equipped to connect your mind and body together.

If you get distracted, don't worry. It's bound to happen, especially in the beginning. However, rather than all your wayward mind to irritate you, just remind yourself of your purpose and redirect it back to the exercise. In time, you'll find that your body and mind will become more in syncwith and you'll find the peace and harmony you're looking for. In time, you'll understand yourself better than you ever thought possible and will be able to handle stressful situations much better than you thought you could.

Chapter Seven: Stop Running in Circles

Mindfulness can be very effective for even more serious behavioral problems. While some cases are very extreme and may require additional treatment, learning how to interrupt intrusive thoughts that may trigger obsessive habits, can literally feel like magic water poured on a tired soul.

For those who struggle with obsessive-compulsive disorder the world may at times feel like it is closing in on you. If left untreated, in time, you may find yourself hiding away from the world into a lonely cocoon of hibernation.

For most of us, obsessive thoughts can take hold of our minds from time to time, but for those with OCD, the thought grabs hold and never lets go. Gradually, they become much more intense until they reach a point where we have lost complete control over everything in our lives.

To combat these thoughts, we really have to return to the basics and really understand what's at the heart of what drives us to do this type of behavior.

Conscious or Subconscious

Our minds are by far the most powerful machinery in the world. With the ability to conjure up as many as 70,000 separate thoughts in a single day, your mind is producing a new thought approximately once every other second. Those numbers apply to the average Joe, not some proficient astro-scientist or savant. Who knows how many thoughts they can come up with. But if you take that to the other end of the spectrum, those with OCD tend to have more thoughts than anyone else. And with understanding that, you begin to grasp the scope of the challenges faced by those with this difficult disorder.

What does this mean? Remember, the subconscious mind is the undercurrent for everything the brain receives from birth onward. It is an impressive machine for receiving and deciphering informationand there is no way to stoptheflow of informationcoming in. However, with OCD, it is not the subconscious mind that is causing this information overload. Instead, it is the conscious mind, the part of the mind responsible for reasoning and logic that is stuck in overdrive. So, if the average person is creating about 70,000 thoughts a day, the person with anxiety disorders like OCD is fighting to keep down a lot more. The good news is that because the problem lies in the conscious mind, there is something you can do about it.

Often the human mind is likened to an iceberg. What we really see is only a part of who we are, so much more lies beneath the surface and is buried under years of indoctrination, fears, and misguided beliefs. The cure for what ails us is usually buried somewhere deep in that quagmire of thoughts that we are fighting against everyday waiting in the fabric of our own mind. So basically, we need to tap into our subconscious to help us fight the battle.

The most effective way to do this is through mindfulness meditation. Each time we have a mindfulness session, we are taking the time to dig deep into the inner recesses of our mind to learn something new about ourselves. Remember, one of the key phases of mindfulness is awareness. We will learn what makes us tick, what triggers our emotions, and what stirs inside of us that compels us to engage in your compulsive behavior. Over time, this type of meditation will pave over the rough patches in our brain and even create new pathways to get us to a preferred destination.

As you become more aware of how your mind works, you develop a sort of intricate wisdom that begins to separate you from your thoughts. You learn to see them as a separate entity, and once that happens, and your personal responsibility is severed, you open the door for a whole new way to respond to the stimulus that is invading your senses. When your thoughts no longer hold you prisoner, you will become more creative, more relaxed, and by extension more successful. All of this will lead you to better health and happiness overall. So, now that you understand the basic mechanism behind reversing your thoughts, let's practice a few exercises to change the script that is running in your head. As you go through the following exercises, your goal is to learn what you believe deep down inside and then develop a strategy to change that belief into something more positive.

Exercise #1

After you've completed your breathing exercises and started to relax:

- Close your eyes and begin to shut out everything around you so you can focus clearly on your own thoughts.
- Take a neutral position in your mind and then start to take notice of each thought you have.
- Notice how that thought makes you feel and what kind of reaction is triggered. Are they upsetting, confusing, or are they disappointing?
- Do not judge the thought as good or bad, but rather just observe them as a neutral party.
- Acknowledge the thought but nothing more.
- Now, switch your focus to something else.

Did you notice anything when you switched your focus? The needling thought that has been bugging you all along usually evaporates or it starts to lose its hold on you. That is a normal mental reaction. When our mind struggles with something, we may have the inclination to fight it with all our strength, but the more we try to fight it, the stronger it gets. If you just ignore the thought and focus your attention on something else, the thought will lose its power and you claim back your mind.

You can view it like you would a game of tug of war with your mind. When you play tug of war with someone, there is constant pressure on both ends. The harder you pull, the harder your opponent pulls. When you play this kind of game with your mind, your mind is always going to win. It has been building up strength for this fight since your first thought. But you can easily end the game by just dropping the rope and letting go of the triggering thought.

Of course, reading this here in this book sounds over simplified. After all, if it was as simple as changing your mind then you would have done that long ago, right? This is very true, however, if you continue with this practice, you will eventually find that thought will slowly start to fade in the background and eventually, it will subside enough for you to reclaim your life back and break free from those compulsive impulses. You're learning how to drop the rope.

Exercise #2

Another mindfulness exercise that works well with OCD is to challenge the thought. Rather than switch your thought to something else, you can:

- Acknowledge the thought
- Then challenge it by asking it a question
- Choose how to react
- Follow through with a different response

When choosing a question to challenge the thought, observe the reality of a situation. Analyze your options before proceeding. It might best be understood with an example.

Suppose you have an obsessive compulsion for washing your hands. Every time you touch something new, you feel a strong urge to wash your hands. As you start your mindfulness exercise, your observations reveal that you have an abnormal fear of bacteria.

Your Mind: If I don't wash my hands, I'll get sick

Your Challenge: But you just washed your hands five minutes ago, how can you get new bacteria if you haven't touched anything?

Or you might ask, what are you missing by spending all your time washing your hands?

Your skin will dry out, it wastes unnecessary time.

Chances are you are missing out on something. It could be a TV program you like, time with your family, or just a chance to spend time with friends. The main idea is that you can use those values, those things you hold near and dear to your heart to challenge your thought process, giving you a very real chance to at the very least, break the hold it has on you and provide some relief. In time, those challenges will mount up and eventually you can break your OCD habits.

It is important to point out here that these are just some basic techniques for dealing with Obsessive-Compulsive Disorder. Many people are able to work these out on their own, but there are also many cases where professional guidance in this and other types of disorders may also be needed. If you find that using OCD techniques is not helping, then it might be best to reach out for additional help in coping with your problem.

Chapter Eight: Running Into the Fray

Another time to turn to mindfulness is when you have to face something unpleasant in your life. No matter who we are, unnerving things happen to us all the time. Every day we wake up we have to face our fears, listen to disturbing news, or otherwise manage things that make us feel extremely uncomfortable. It may be a death in the family, dealing with sickness, or it may be something that forces us to face our own personal turmoil.

Dealing with these things can conjure up some of the most negative emotions we can possibly feel. In fact, they can become so intense that if not addressed, they could easily cause our physical bodies to begin to disintegrate. We fall apart, we collapse, and we become ill ourselves. In the end, we are left thoroughly spent, exhausted from the fight.

The inclination here is to fight against it. To push that anxiety deep down in our soul and try to keep the feelings from coming out. Whether you're experiencing anxiety, fear, depression, or some other negative emotion, it doesn't feel good so you fight against it. However, if you can take a few minutes to practice some of these mindfulness techniques, you'll be amazed how they will infuse you with the strength to push through the bad stuff and come out on the other side feeling more powerful than ever.

The Three Breath Hug

This technique is very effective in grounding you in the moment. Unlike the other meditation practices we've discussed in this book, this one needs to be done with someone else. We all know how good it feels to get a hug from others, by adding a hugging meditation practice to your stressful days, you can actually experience an emotional transformation.

When you hug another person, the hearts connect and the two of you for the moment become one. By the time you pull apart, you will be more in sync with each other. When you add mindful concentration, the healing process begins. In fact, experts point out that hugging can actually decrease stress levels and slow down the heart rate, which often speeds up when you're dealing with fear and anxiety.

- Start by standing face-to-face with another person
- Bow your head to acknowledge the other person
- Begin your breathing exercise
- Approach the other person for a hug
- Embrace the other and hold for three breaths
  * The first breath is to acknowledge your presence in the embrace
  * The second breath is to acknowledge the presence and contribution of the other person
  * On the third breath, focus your attention on being happy for the union
- Pull apart
- Bow again to the other party
- Finally, express your gratitude for the other person

Sorting Boxes

- Start by focusing on your breathing without attempting to change it. So, if your breathing is agitated when you begin, just accept and acknowledge it

- Take note of any feelings you might have – these could include any sensations, emotions, anxiety, etc. Your goal is to increase awareness of how your body is responding at that specific point in time.
- Close your eyes
- Visualize three boxes in your mind:
    * The first box is for your thoughts
    * The second is for your sensations
    * The third is for your emotions
- Begin to mentally sort anything that comes into your mind and put them in the appropriate boxes

When you do this exercise you will soon realize that you are better able to clear your head of those negative feelings and sensations. You will no longer find yourself worrying about the past or dreading the future but will be better equipped to focus on the here and now. You'll find that once you shed the negative feelings and thoughts, your mood will improve and you'll feel invigorated.

Chapter Nine: Embracing the Good

The secret to the success of mindfulness is that it teaches you how to love yourself. So often, we allow our inner critic to dictate how to feel and how to act. We may start out consciously working towards a positive goal, but somewhere along the way, that inner demon gets the better of us and with its insistent needling compels us to take a detour. Practicing mindfulness is really learning the art of showing love for ourselves. It stops us from constantly reliving our past mistakes, worrying about what might have been, or in some way convincing ourselves that we are not deserving.

When we allow our minds to engage in endless worries, it not only robs us of our precious time and energy, it takes away our joy, a commodity that is already in short supply in this world. Take a moment right now contemplate what it would mean for you to live only in the present. Without any thought to what has already happened in the past or what you might expect from the future. To live for right now.

If we learn to do this, we won't feel guilty about doing the things we truly love. There is a reason why you need to embrace your passions without the feeling of shame and guilt. These are the tools you need to rejuvenate your spirit so that you can charge into another day of chaos. Your passions are the things that make it possible for you to develop that kind of tunnel vision that allows you to be in the moment. Forcing yourself into a mold that doesn't feel right is what gives us anxiety or leads us into depression. By embracing the good, we learn to love ourselves and to do the things that make us feel good.

This is not to encourage you to avoid responsibility. We all have to maintain some level of balance and none of us can expect to do everything we want to do all the time. However, if you learn how to love yourself enough to use those things you have passion for to help you course correct, you'll be much better equipped to handle the responsible and less enjoyable things in your life much easier. So, when you want to foster more positivity in your life, try some of these exercises to put you on the right track.

The Checker

When you are busy in the throes of your day, always do a mental check-in to make sure you're still aware of your surroundings. If you are carefully observant of your thoughts, you will notice the point when they begin to turn negative. When this happens try taking the following steps:

- See the thought as a neutral party without judgment
- Label the thought as negative
- Remind yourself that your brain has many functions and one area is specifically designed for checking facts
- Visualize a machine checking facts
- Now, visualize the machine is malfunctioning and observe the negative thought as it is damaged by the machine.
- Give yourself permission to turn the machine off

Change Gears

You can also do repeat the same exercise we learned in the last chapter. When you notice your thoughts are turning negative, do not accept them. Instead, shift your focus to something else. When you can do that, your thoughts can no longer have the power it once had.

Conclusion

The ability to control the thoughts that flow through your mind is just another form of self-discipline, but it goes far beyond that. If you want to achieve something, if you want to excel at anything you do, you must first learn how to redirect that inner voice that is always sabotaging your happiness. But you can't change something if you can't identify it. That's where mindfulness can be a major help.

Think about it. If someone asked you to turn off the light switch, you would first need to find out where the switch is. Then you would need to understand the kind of switch it is and how to turn it off. But if it were in a place you'd never been before, you'd have to go exploring. You'd probably run your hands along the walls in the darkness until you felt something that resembled a switch. You'd manipulate for a while to see if it is the right switch. If you were unsuccessful, then you would go exploring in the darkness once again.

Mindfulness is like that. We should all be familiar with the voices inside our heads, but we've allowed the pressures of this world to take hold of us and move us along like robots. When we first begin mindfulness we're in unfamiliar territory. The exercises may seem strange in the beginning. You might even feel a little self-conscious and embarrassed, but in time, you'll fall right into it. As you learn more and more about your own body, the more intrigued you will be and you'll be drawn to explore your inner self in even more depth. It'll be like turning on the light in a dark room and seeing who you really are for the first time. Some of us will like what we see while others will want to make major changes. No matter what your goals are, mindfulness will help you get there.

All of us want the best out of life, we just don't know how to aquire it. Or they just don't know how much effort is involved in getting to their destination. We are stronger than we think we are, and once we break free of our inner critic, we'll find there is a whole lot more fight left in us than we thought we had. Once you realize that you can do more, do better, that inner dialogue will start to change, and you'll be able to push yourself far beyond the limits you've set for yourself.

Throughout your life, you'll have many friends come and go. They will be good for a while, but into time the will move on with their lives. Few of us have friends that will stick with us throughout our lifetimes so why not become your own best friend. You are the only person that will stick with you through thick and thin. That you can trust and rely on. Mindfulness will help you to see your own potential and help you draw a roadmap on how to get there.

Today's reality gives evidence that we have no idea what our true potential really is. We live in a cushy world of comfort that no previous generation ever had. Few of us are willing to test ourselves to find out what we really can do, and even fewer see the need to do so. But how much more rewarding can your life be if you incorporate more of the real you into it?

We hope that you have gleaned valuable insight from this book. It doesn't matter what your goals in life are, it is your mindset that will get your there. It is your perception of yourself and world around you that dictates what you make of the life you have.

It will take time, but if you do it, and do it regularly, the results you get from practicing mindfulness will be more than enough to provide you with amazing benefits physically, emotionally, mentally, and even spiritually.

So, now, stop reading this book and go and get to know yourself.

Journal Exercises

The following pages have been designed to get you to start mindfulness practice. You will notice that each question will be a follow-up question to the one before. This is a progressive method so that each time you complete a page, you'll be learning how to think even more deeply. This will help you to get the most benefit out of your mindfulness practice from the very start. While you will not need to spend hours pouring over these questions taking valuable time away from other important activities. It is a good idea for you to dedicate at least ten to fifteen minutes each day to this type of mindfulness practice.

Day 1

What are my predominant thoughts?

Why?

Day 2

What am I doing when these thoughts come up. What are my triggers?

Day 3

What kind of things bring me a sense of calm?

Day 4

What kinds of things cause me fear? Why?

Day 5

Which of my fears are based in reality?

Day 6

How are those fears holding me back?

Day 7

What can I do when I feel stressed?

Day 8

List new habits that can make you more mindful

Day 9

If I could go back in time, what advice would I give to my younger self?

Day 10

If there were only 12 hours to a day, what would be my priority?

Day 11

List 5 ways being kinder to others will boost your own self-esteem

Day 12

What past negative experiences keep coming up in your mind? Name three ways to challenge those thoughts.

Day 13

Name past experiences you missed out on because of negative thoughts. How did you miss out? How can you change?

Day 14

What habits do you have that are actually avoidance tactics?

Day 15

If you could change one negative in your life, what would it be?

Day 16

What physical reactions do you have from negative thoughts?

Day 17

List ten ways you will show gratitude in the future

Day 18

What do you think people expect from you? What can you deliver?

Day 19

Who are the toxic people in your life?

Why?

Day 20

What can you do when your thoughts get out of control?

Day 21

What is your strongest emotion? Why?

Day 22

What exercises can you do at night to ensure better sleep?

Day 23

What are your short-term and long-term goals? What steps can you take to achieve them?

Day 24

What is keeping you from living in the moment?

Day 25

What repetitive mistakes are you making most often? Why?

Day 26

What things would you like your inner voice to say?

Day 27

List ways you can become kinder to yourself.

Day 28

How can you have a better relationship with yourself?

Day 29

How are you making your own life more difficult? List ways you can change it.

Day 30

What is your inner creator?

Imprint